A Thousand Questions

poems by

Iris Gersh

Finishing Line Press
Georgetown, Kentucky

A Thousand Questions

To my family, especially my nieces and sister, and all my friends who supported me in publishing my first book. To all the people globally who died or became ill from the Coronavirus, and those they left behind. To the firefighters fighting in California, Oregon, Washington state, and Colorado. To all the caring, kind, and strong people who contribute to saving America and who work for social, racial, gender, and environmental justice.

Copyright © 2020 by Iris Gersh
ISBN 978-1-64662-360-0 First Edition
All rights reserved under International and Pan-American Copyright Conventions. No part of this book may be reproduced in any manner whatsoever without written permission from the publisher, except in the case of brief quotations embodied in critical articles and reviews.

ACKNOWLEDGMENTS

"Like a Gregorian Chant" and "Gala Room" appear in *Fixed and Free Poetry Anthology*, 2018, 10th Anniversary Edition, Editor and Publisher, Billy Brown.

"Catskills, the Fifties" appears in *Manzano Mountain Review* Issue #1: Winter 2017 online.

"Shhhh, Don't Let the String Hear You" was published in *Shadow of the Snake*, from a reading at the Rattlesnake Museum, May 2015, Poetry Playhouse Publications, Albuquerque.

"Unplugged" and "Stains" appear in *Fixed and Free Poetry Anthology*, 2015, Editor and Publisher, Billy Brown.

Publisher: Leah Huete de Maines
Editor: Christen Kincaid
Cover Art: Iris Gersh
Author Photo: Denise Gordon
Cover Design: Elizabeth Maines McCleavy

Order online: www.finishinglinepress.com
        also available on amazon.com

Author inquiries and mail orders:
Finishing Line Press
P. O. Box 1626
Georgetown, Kentucky 40324
U. S. A.

Table of Contents

Like a Gregorian Chant 1

High Holy Days 3

Reverence 5

Catskills, the Fifties 6

Mahogany Night Stick 7

Grandma Rebecca 8

Randy, the Girl Next Door 9

Grew Up on Della Reese 10

Shhhh, Don't Let the String Hear You 11

Happenings, the Sixties 12

Comfort Over Style 13

Ouzo-Driven 15

Unplugged 16

Sometimes a Waste of Time 18

Den Pai 20

Stripping the Olives 21

Black Magic 22

Sto Kato-Kato, Poiós Noiázetai? 24

Stains, *a Ghazal* 25

Archaeological Love, *a Pantoum* 26

Crazy Women 27

Returning 28

A Night Star Blanches the Turnips 29

Your Teeth 30

Gala Room 31

Fear in America 32

Catskill Grey 34

LIKE A GREGORIAN CHANT

In the taverna, safe
at our table, my boyfriend and I raise
glasses of *retsina*, salute
men at other tables.
One man, his black hair
dusted with snow, sings,

his *cavatina* filling the room,
another answers, three
join the chorus swell
till a round of voices
asks, answers, echoing
monastic ceremonies.

The tavern keeper pulls out
two grills of roasted lamb
from the firepit, fills
tin jugs with wine,
pushes a log into the fire.
It is hushed now as we eat and drink.

Witness to something sacred,
my selvaged thoughts unraveled,
I lapse into the secular, imagine
the pleasure of licking,
with my wine-sweetened tongue,
the lips of the youngest man,
alone at a faraway table, imagine

unwinding sheep-colored
skeins that sit in the lap
of the tavern keeper's wife,
my claws newly sharpened, imagine

my voice joining the men's,
my song the blues, my company
wailing guitars and harmonica riffs.

Then frightened by this
private irreverence, I stand
by the open window,
look down at the village clock
whose face snow softly covers,
the only number visible, one.

HIGH HOLY DAYS

The air reeks of old—
old people and
stale breath from the night before
when fasting began.

On Yom Kippur morning,
the few scattered Jewish families
from town congregate at the
Colonial Hotel and Motel,
across our road, Route 209.

We gather in the makeshift temple,
converted from the hotel camp's playroom
where on summer days tourist children
run in and out, picking through old games and crafts.

Today the *shul* is occupied by rows of chairs,
men sitting on one side, and women on the other,
all dressed in somber colors, mourning the dead.

My brother, sister, and I find places
to sit where we can see one another,
and try to keep from cracking up as
the rabbi drones on in Hebrew.

Suddenly he wails, reminding us
of the call of the *shofar* on Rosh Hashonah,
nine days earlier when we began the week of
reflection, when we asked to be forgiven and
to be inscribed in the Book of Life.

Once the congregants pray, chant and mumble,
as if on cue, we children escape,
sneak into the hotel's kitchen,
grab a few chicken legs, intent on breaking the fast
way before sundown.

This was not the first year
we decided the High Holy Days were only for adults,
only the first year we have sinned. We run home to eat,
then get rid of the evidence in hopes we will be forgiven.

REVERENCE

for the way the dancers at the Kewa Pueblo
shake their corn rattles,
for the way their families eat Twinkies,
their brown bodies gleaming in the fall sun,
for the way the women wear *tablitas*, turquoise
three-pointed wooden headpieces and long velvet
skirts, bells jingling with each step they take,

for the way chants circle the world
from the Gregorian chants of the monks
to the *salsa* rhythms to the *davening*,
prayers the cantors sing, to songs we hear now,
sung by men in powwow drum circles,

for the way we join our fingers together,
we do not get on our knees or enter houses of prayers—
instead we open our mouths, tap our feet,

for the way we let the corn's source,
the ground's blood as it runs through and underneath,
we let the source enter us, an unending pulse,

for the mesa where the sun sinks behind purple mountains,
in another place so we can sleep,
sounds of drums coursing through our blood,
the desire to stop asking so many questions leaving us.

CATSKILLS, the Fifties

My sister and I swing on the hammock,
ignoring our father's curses
when a pot of corn boils over,
corn gathered that morning
from the field behind our backyard,
then husked in strong pulls.

Traffic whizzes by on Route 209—
from New York City, green and white buses
of Hasidic Jews, dressed dark, warm,
escaping to bungalow colonies, other buses
of Blacks in summer whites, cool,
en route to Peg Leg Bates Motel where
my cool brother and his friends sneak into.

Prison workers across the road pick
different corn, other families' meals,
and I imagine they watch us,
plan to get in our house at night
while we sleep.

Our luxury of self-imposed stillness,
my sudden fear never voiced,
is broken now by my mother's call,
"come inside, set the table, and
leave your father alone".

I arrange lilac flowers
in a Chinese vase, soft order,
the only noise, dogs barking
at an itinerant on the road,
the setting sun passing his shadow
across the now empty hammock.

MAHOGANY NIGHT STICK

hangs on a large nail by the inside door.
Snowy weather makes us rush inside, in seconds
enveloped by heat that steams my glasses.

Night stick, warning or threat
to someone who breaks into the house,
disturbs our peace.

Solid dark night stick, a symbol
of my father's power to keep control.
Times he'll pick it up and say he'll beat
the "living crap" out of my rebellious
teenage brother.

The space holds no more than two of us,
and snow-covered boots, Dad's work shoes,
outerwear stuffed into a closet.

Stifled, crowded, hungry from smells of chicken and potatoes
wafting from the kitchen, we are raring to go up the three steps.

I inherited the night stick, kept it in Florida,
lost it in Greece, and in New Mexico, a co-worker
made me one from a sawed-off shovel,
to protect me when I slid in the icy parking lot
at the State Capitol late at night after my shift.

My father radiated anger. After he died, well-meaning friends
called him by the correct lay-language name, a rageaholic.
His own words seemed to swell up from way inside him,
taught us how to express rage, to spew profanities.

My father hurt my brother and my sister
never with weapons, but with his words.
They could not be bullied, only bore the brunt
of his attacks while I was spared till later.

If I hold the stick even now, I hold
its power and its tempered strength.

GRANDMA REBECCA

I remember visits to my grandmother in the Bronx,
on Southern Boulevard. In the '57 forest green Chevy, we giggled
and ate stale red licorice while my parents fought,
my mother giving directions to my obstinate father.

We raced up the steps in the piss-smelly halls.
I remember Grandma Rebecca's broad smile when she saw us,
my parents, my brother, sister and me.

We could not understand the Yiddish she and my father spoke.
Maybe a few words we recognized, like *shayna maidelah*, good girls.
How was it good though that Grandma Rebecca was afraid all the time
since her place was robbed a few days earlier,
> when they locked her in the hallway closet till she was almost lost
> amid the cleaning supplies and heavy coats, till Uncle Morris
> tripped over a step ladder to find her silent and weeping?

I remember her brown serene face and the softest hands, always
folded in her lap, as we waited until my Uncle Louie, bent over, so
meek, and his wife Lili with her made up face and loud good nature,
arrived with the food: corned beef and pastrami sandwiches,
potato salad, kosher pickles, and chopped liver and bags of
rugelach. We, who never ate deli in the country, gorged and
belched it up with cream soda.

After we left, I remember my parents fighting in this strange new
language, not only about directions but also about *tsorris*, important
family troubles.

RANDY, THE GIRL NEXT DOOR

choppy hair framing her face,
patters around the inside of her family's garage.
My sister and I let her be the mother.
"Be good!" her tiny voice commands
as she hands us the lipstick tube.
We obey, smear Crimson Creme on our lips,
follow her example, await the next direction.

Her skinny body totters on three-inch heels.
Her shriek penetrates the rafters when she thinks
we make fun of her, but when we curtsy and smile,
she waves fake red fingernails at her good children,
climbs onto a rocker, and pulls stuffing out of a doll.
Fluff flies onto our hair, sticks to our mouths,
then settles on the player piano.

GREW UP ON DELLA REESE

before she was touched by any angel.
"I've got my love to keep me warm,"
she sang while my father reclined,
warmed up by her and in equal bliss by

Lena Horne, sleek and cool in music and looks.
My dad forgot his backbreaking plumbing work.

Dinah Washington sang about the leaves of brown
tumbling down. We sang together.
"Do you remember that September in the rain?"

Who was his muse when he painted everything
fire-engine orange in the kitchen,
toaster, pencil sharpener, bread box?
Who inspired my father?

Maybe Keely Smith, a country gal who
married her partner, Louis Prima, after
he scooped her up as his singer, then subjugated
her energy, her personality, to his.
"When day is done, I think of all the joys we knew."

Keely Smith, Prima's sidekick, her deadpan expression set in
just so much stone as he upstaged her on variety shows, and
tried to suppress her, emerged on top with her sultry voice, her
vitality, her youthful spirit.

Later we watched Sonny and Cher do the same shtick,
Cher standing with her arms crossed, rolling her eyes,
stone-cold, still, waiting for Sonny to stop, just stop,
for an eternity, it seemed, and then together they belted out
music that rocked the early seventies.

"And the beat goes on still moving strong on and on."

SHHHH, DON'T LET THE STRING HEAR YOU

> *"Dangerous animals became even more sinister and uncanny in the night. A snake was never called by its name at night, because it would hear. It was called a 'string'."*
> from *Things Fall Apart* by Chinua Achebe

Brother string uncoils, slides down the arroyo, like a slinky.
Its sister string stays back in the bush, just as fearless, but not
as hungry.
Baby strings hear voices of the crier.
Villagers too hear the crier, his voice mingling with the forest
insects, the air aflame with their trills and chirrups.
Love and potent jungle kola nuts treat spirit affliction.
Cosmic strings travel the same road as the jaguar, the
tarantula, and sometimes, though rarely, a bloodflower.

HAPPENINGS, the Sixties

My brother made twenty gray concrete bulls
out of Plaster of Paris, pasted on our family name,
drew one arrow for each mile leading to our house.
We cruised out early one morning and placed
the bulls in prominent road corners: 44/55, up on 209.

Gersh's college friends descended
like so many brightly feathered birds,
some carrying bottles of wine,
others bongos, guitars, poetry books.

My father stood on the highway,
directed cars to park on the side, away from our house.
A sporty Fiat bypassed him, slid into the garden,
squashing lilies-of-the-valley newly bloomed.
This is one time I remember he checked his anger.

Cauldrons of corn boiled on the brick grill, freshly
picked from the field we rented to the Mahoneys.
A couple made out by the lilac trees
till my father shooed them back to the house
where Bob Dylan blasted from the record player.

My brother appeared only to disappear.
Maybe he figured once he spread the bulls
on the country roads, he could let the rest happen.
My mother told the complaining neighbors to
please come to her son's next happening, that it
might become a family tradition.

COMFORT OVER STYLE

Mom never told us to stay clean, only when to return home.
Behind the cornfield, my sister and I dug out dirt sitting places
for friends after we ran races, then later for my Science Club, open
to other 12-year-old girls who wanted to discover names of bugs and
birds, to pretend we lived in an intellectual world.

Mom wore faded black pedal pushers, strings hanging down her
calves, sewed matching green four-leaf clover tops for the three of us.
She loved dressing up in shiny white sheath dresses and heels when
she ushered at the Woodstock Playhouse or when she and my father
went out.

Years later in Florida where she moved after my father died,
casual clothes suited her fine. She loved her sets of matching velour
hooded tops and pants, in her favorite pastel colors of sea foam green,
coral, lemony yellow. Mom merged with the colors she decorated her
condo with, lavender verticals, magnolias on teal wallpaper, coral
rugs.

She would loan me and my sister her culottes if we walked around the
golf course. Our hair piled atop our heads, we laughed how nerdy we
looked, never denying how comfortable we felt.

In my thirties I still got clothes from my mother, flowery and gaudy.
My style would never evolve if I wore only polyester jogging suits
or terry cloth shorts.

Now my New Mexico denim patchwork skirts and
combat boots belonged to the past.
What happened to my six years as a hippie on Lama Mountain?

My mother convinced me at age 30 to marry.
My intended was cute enough, not a worker though and made no
money at the car wash where I met him, no one who would make
my life easier, leaving me to wonder if I would ever find a man who
would make me happy.

Maybe he was another hand me down, to confirm my mother's belief that I was on track in the world.

OUZO-DRIVEN

For my brother Bill who always told me,
Take no shit from anyone, even him
like when we screamed and there was
no way out in Renee's mother's house
in Florida, and my mother said,
"I didn't raise my children to be barbarians."

It's longer than sundown here in Sofiko.
Are there bigger concerns? Or is it only about
making a salad or asking my man what he needs?

A tribute to ends of days, onions, cigarettes, fire,
a woman ouzo-driven, who has fattened her
nerves, has grown tired of serving.

A woman who is ouzo-hungover has no cares.
She can finally leave.

When she does after eight years,
she mourns wasted passion, the jealousy,
the dragging out of time when she might have forgotten
or at least forgiven him.

She speaks to her man as if he stands in front of her.
She says that maybe what I'm really missing
> Is your country
> Its light
> Its olive smell
> Its hardness

And not you at all.

UNPLUGGED

Skeleton figurines, silhouetted
against a west window,
float astride skeleton horses.

Ceramic hens and roosters
share a window sill with blue glass bottles.
Visiting his house on the mountain reminds me
of our jam sessions where he would play
washtub bass, Annie and I on the inherited
Grand Steinway, playing ragtime.

My brother Bill's geraniums regenerate,
their leaves, soft brown, papyrus-light, fall—and

a deep emptiness unfolds.

Dust flies in, scatters
when someone lifts a tissue out of its box,
or if anyone moves around the art books, or
when the skeletons move.

I leave dead moths on the sill,
under the brim of a still
unclaimed Ecuadorean cowboy hat,
next to broken Florida shells, one
a conch he found in the Keys.

Outside stretch piles and piles
of two-by-fours, quartz rocks, rotting logs
once meant for *vigas*, cracked toilet seats,
clay pottery, the funny duck one for his ashes
Georgia and Rachel, his daughters,
carried from Florida to New Mexico.

Years later, hollyhocks, jonquils, roses, and
purple irises grow alongside the new lilacs, strawberry
bushes, root alongside trees
haphazardly planted during the last
ten years he lived: aspen, willow, a sturdy apple tree
whose green knotted flowers look edible.

SOMETIMES A WASTE OF TIME
In Your Father's Village

You lean over the bed, kiss me awake, you
tasting like your mud-bottomed Greek coffee.
We discuss what I will do today
alone in your father's village.
I want to go to the town where you work,
hang out on the stony beach with tourists.
You tell me I have more to do in the village.

Once you leave, I lie in bed a little longer,
then am content to sit in the sun outside our one room
attached to your father's house.
I wave to the neighbor lady hanging clothes,
the lady who asks a thousand questions,
usually starting with "*Poú eínai óloi?*" Where's everyone? leading up to
"*Thélo kafé!*" She likes how I make it.

I make a list. Lists have always kept me straight.
        Today I will paint the brown ceiling white,
           walk to the store for bread,
             cinnamon, something sweet,
                and make rabbit stew for the first time.
I will not think about the rabbit stew.

I add with stars ****go to the post office and wonder
what the men think of me, the *Amerikana* who belongs to her Greek.

After the errands, I arrive at home to find a group of women
gathered outside at our table and benches,
tiny-stitched needlepoint and crocheting projects in their laps.
I attempt to patch a hole in your old workpants,
offer them orange drinks and smiles. First annoyed, I
appreciate that these women make an effort to care about me.

When they leave, I heat a five-gallon water can
on the two-burner stove for your shower.
Later, I will dump your dirty water in the unplanted field.
Then when you tell me the rabbit stew isn't done and ask me
why I don't know how to cook, I keep it to myself that I will not always
pass my days in these sewing circles, always smiling politely.

DEN PAI

"*Den pai*," it doesn't go, she says when I take her crocheted table cover and with care lie it on the rough white table (in our bathroom), then decorate with American woman tchotchkes—a wooden crane, a fringed tie-dyed scarf folded into a random bowl, a framed photo of my mother and me. "*Den pai*," she says when I am ready to add carrots to the lentils on the stove, says it twice, like ABSOLUTELY *den pai*. She throws in words I hear many times while I live there, *pou apagorévontai* (you are forbidden!). I am terribly sorry, you are not my mother, and you are nasty to boot, carrots do pai, they do go, get a bowl of lentils just about anywhere except here in Greece, and carrots are ubiquitous. So there! In my hausfrau life, I have not forgotten that fake flowers are symbolic of fake people. I remove them from all surfaces and hide them way up on the top of the kitchen shelves, joining my many photo albums (my past life hidden from view). Any time I leave, she puts them back.

STRIPPING THE OLIVES
In Your Mother's Village

After lunch, the women workers separate olives,
branches, and leaves left on the *strómas* spread on the ground.
Legs stretched out in front of me, next to your squatting mother,
I raise my head to see you high in another laden tree.
I am as bare as the tree when you finish stripping its olives.
The small red rake works well.

I'm glad I have stayed, this harvest
the first time I feel useful, as if I am at last giving
back to your family who even now helps
me lift heavy burlap bags.

I smell lamb we grilled for lunch,
its burnt odor carried by the ocean breeze.
On my tongue remains the bitter taste of *retsina*
we drank. My hands are stained purple
with juice of bruised olives.

The priest, your cousin, arrives, taking care his black robe skirts
broken stones scattered in piles. Your mother and aunt,
their raw words slicing the air, ignore his pleas for peace.
You tell me this is how it is every year,
the two sisters fighting. Stones no longer serve
as a boundary between each woman's property.
Next to theirs, our quarrels seem tame.

I move away to sit alone in a sun-shimmered spot.
Knowledge of life's continuity replenishes me.
I am no longer the stripped olive tree.

Your calling my name sounds tender in the olive grove.
It is quiet now. The women move to the next tree, spread out
the net blankets that will catch the falling olives.
Before you climb the ladder again, we kiss, our lips
touching softly like the distant sounds of sheep bells.

BLACK MAGIC

Sunday morning in Sofiko. Its name could mean
power, maybe craziness as the birds go berserk.
Rose petals have flown off the bushes,
blown into the yard to join bushels of leaves.

I want to be here more than every three weeks,
away from the drama of Korinthos, away from the mother.

Under an apricot tree, my boyfriend hammers away on
the outdoor grill. Pieces of wood stick out against the blue sky,
concrete crumbles around its base. It could be an electric chair
prototype or perhaps a large King's throne.

The one working phone in Sofiko has painted white keys, its harlequin theme punctuated with broken words, scratched with broken glass in rusty metal—where a Sofiko citizen teen etched "Sofico City" and some Greek words.

Later my lover says that those words mean, "I fuck the house,"
and I ask, what does that even mean?
I ask myself, what made me think we could be a couple?

The main street in Sofiko is empty at night,
not like during the day when I greet and am greeted, and
even as different as I am from the people here, they always
treat me warmly, always helpful, interested in me, offering
a warm baklava and a cup of inviting bubbling Greek coffee.

Now at night, I feel vulnerable like the time I am told to
hitchhike to Almiri, and I get a ride with someone in the Navy who
tells me we could be friends. "Do you know what being friends means?"
I end up questioning him about all his ports of call, inside swearing
at my boyfriend whose lazy ass, whose interest in everything and
everyone except me, has led me into a car with a new friend.

A Satan star symbol covers the space above the phone booth.

People practice black magic in Sofiko.
Once I told the neighbor lady, Katerina, about a dead fish floating
next to me in Katakali. She said that I should have taken it out
of the water, dead or not, I should have brought it to her.
She points her finger, shaking her head from side to side, saying *neh,
neh*, yes, yes, as her kerchief flies into our yard.

Now at the end of the road, I hear my mother's sweet voice on the
Satan phone. I'm calling from Sofiko, I say, then speak louder
as I finger circles and pentangles on the glass wall in the Hell booth.
She asks me where the goats are, the rooster that she usually hears
when I call her. No, ma, it's night in the village, pitch black, and so
many stars.

STO KATO-KATO, POIÓS NOIÁZETAI?
"In the end who cares?"

Two brooms, a yellow soppy mop
balance against the black gate we painted.
Grills with residue of too tough lamb
hang on the daphne tree, its bay leaves shriveled.

A pitchfork leans into an unsprung mattress.
My sister's bleached white shorts hang on the clothesline
alongside large balls of mizithra cheese, almost ready.
Garlic bunches are strung from a pole.

What's steady here?
What doesn't lean, or hang, or
need to be strung?

It is quiet with only
the sound of wind through the cypresses.
A few heavy *stafillia* plop onto the flagstone.
Black birds' wings flutter as the birds swoop
to pick up the grapes.

A door slams, meaning he is home, and
the muscles in my back tense.
If I move, I feel pain.

What do you want? he asks,
He acts like his reading my emotions matters.
Sometimes, I answer, I want to go to the beach.
Louise says she needs a nap.

Chickens he forgot about in his bag
squawk, indignant for being forgotten.
Their hysteria catches till tears roll down our eyes.

Later we make a fire indoors and cedar logs
sputter and groan.

STAINS, *a Ghazal*

His lighters and matchboxes contain revealing smears.
Splotches of coffee and wine stains explain past years.

Like solace for leftover lovers sweetened by time,
his bride believes she alone reigns during his final years.

A blind lover proclaims her hand still burns, that
places she touched him are a refrain to her scarred years.

His wine-soaked spirit reflects in their love-saturated eyes.
His blood courses in their veins till they spurt the years.

No one knows how long it has been since his death.
The goddess of the rainbow remains for eternal years.

ARCHAEOLOGICAL LOVE, *a Pantoum*

Discarded love,
Look at the source: potsherds of no archeological value,
Shards in my garden
Broken, smashed, formless pottery.

Look at the source: potsherds of no archeological value,
Unglazed unfinished pieces
Broken, smashed, formless pottery.
Throwaway love.

Unglazed unfinished pieces
Lovers we never honored,
Throwaway love
Yet hard to throw away.

Lovers we never honored,
Shards in my garden.
Hard to throw away.
Is it possible to explore other archaeological sites?

CRAZY WOMEN

A friend of mine,
more manic than depressive,
bought three hundred dollars
of marine equipment, and
never owned a boat.

Another woman, while in a car
with me from California
to New Mexico, sucked straight from
a can of processed cheese,
the empty nozzle sound driving me crazy
on the six-lane highway, and crazier still
when she told me to pull over so she could meditate.

In the South End of Boston, pre-gentrified,
drunk women draped over parked cars,
figures among shrouded-in-snow Victorian lamp lights.
They talked to themselves or anyone who would listen.
Could it take much to go over that edge?
I remember thinking then.

Some of their mouths twitched
as if they had so much more to say.
They contorted their hands
as if they might never touch again.
Some disappeared like Eve's footsteps
when she grabbed the half-eaten apple
and ran away from the rib-giver.

Crazy women no longer seem outsiders,
isolated wisps atop mountain peaks.
Sometimes now I visit their world,
a place without geography,
not unknowingly, not unwillingly,
just to twitch, contort, and disappear.

RETURNING

Chamisa roasts in the afternoon sun
its yellow flowers turning October brown.
I gather with six other women to share
        contents of our journals.

We lower ourselves rung by rung
from the loft in a geodesic dome at Lama Foundation,
a mile up the road from D.H. Lawrence's shrine.

I have returned to the Sangre de Cristo mountains
to celebrate my 40th birthday and quitting smoking,
and to take a journal workshop with Kay Leigh Hagan.

Mountains vibrate with sounds of wolves and spirits,
        and I wonder where to look first:

close to my feet at the sagebrush
which opens up the breathing passages
and slows down the rush, or
across to the Rio Grande Gorge,
a chasm of infinite space.

Beauty this deep opens up the imagination.
An elk's bugle cry sounds like a *shofar*
        announcing the start of a new year.

Beauty this deep also lays bare our limitations.
Who are we as we stand among the piñon trees
        frozen in the windless night?
Are we seven sisters trying to identify seven in the sky?
Clouds cover the stars tonight, so tomorrow the Pleiades.
It seems enough that we are here, together, and I—home.
Inside, the fire blazes. We put aside our journals
        and play gin rummy until daylight comes.

A NIGHT STAR BLANCHES TURNIPS

She tugs carrots and turnips
out of the high desert ground.

Night sky's blackness,
its Milky Way
creamy phosphorescence,
invites planters like her
to search for one perfect
shooting star.

She fingers purple spheres,
brushes away dirt
to reveal roots,
fine fibrous specimens,
remarkable, she thinks,
how they hold these plants.

She covers her crop
carefully with thick tarps, and
climbs the wooden ladder to her home.

As she sleeps, she dreams a night star
shoots into the garden,
its light exploding
onto the pile.

Her turnips create new soil,
their roots spreading deeper
till the chill air warms with
morning sun rising above the
Sangre de Cristos.

YOUR TEETH
(first poem I read in Albuquerque at a poetry reading)

You get older, and you think about dentures.
You find a receipt for clindamycin, the tooth antibiotic, the dentist prescribes before pulling a tooth.
You're surprised he only gives you Tylenol #3. A friend tells you that is one drug that's passé for pain.
You start thinking about "partial dentures," you think about a health care system that doesn't take care of our teeth.
You think you got the wrong tooth pulled. That's scary cause the one next to it is more visible. You may be older, but you are still a little vain.
You start reading about how dental bacteria goes into your blood, your heart, and can make you sicker and maybe even KILL YOU.
You imagine your heart beating faster. You imagine your organs disintegrating along with rotting teeth.
You think about Juarez. A friend of yours drives Isleta Casino employees down to El Paso. One time, her friend had all her teeth pulled and a complete set of dentures set up in half a day. Done. Her pain was so bad Carlota told the dentist "give her more morphine." That was her hardest run.
Your sister says, "If you go to Juarez, I'll disown you as my sister."
Your mother always said to take care of your teeth.
You pressure your local clinic to put out chairs for their patients.
To get there at 5 a.m. and sit on the floor is disgraceful. The story makes it into the Albuquerque Journal and features Drew, the best community dentist ever. A company brings in chairs. You feel that we are not powerless. You feel it is not only about your teeth anymore.
You shouldn't smoke. Ruins the gums. You shouldn't eat a coffee nip before sleeping. You floss and pic and use ACT mouthwash to protect against cavities. You stop using your teeth to rip open plastic wrappers.

GALA ROOM

> *Poets and community gather on a hot July day in honor of*
> *Simon Ortiz, and in respect for the cultures that built and lived at*
> *Casa San Ysidro, formerly the Gutiérrez House in Corrales.*
> *Dr. Ward Alan Minge employed members of the Acoma tribe he*
> *had befriended.*

We are cooled by the floor's large shale slabs
from the pueblo, dusted with cottonwood's "cotton,"
not unlike dirty white fluffs of sheep's wool on the table in the
weaving room next door.

Adobe walls are almost a foot in thickness.
Vigas and latillas differ in shapes and sizes.
Latillas merge into shapes of the thunderbird,
up and down and sideways. If the ceiling
were broken by summer hailstorms, lightning bolts
would cross the thundering sky.

The Courtyard must have been the
Minges' delight as it cools down in the
evening just as the cicadas
begin their incessant chirping,
a constant refrain of life, a staccato
alert—wake up, wake up, wake up.

We congregate in the courtyard, at ease and energized
by sharing and the special history of Casa San Ysidro.

Acoma Shale
Courtyard's Shade
keep us centered and cool.

FEAR IN AMERICA

America never could own up to who lived here first
never could call Pilgrims immigrants.
Instead we filled history books with lies, or worse,
    we left out the truth, omissions that formed
    children's beliefs.

Public lands became privatized, cut into for oil drilling,
fracking as if the environment is not terrible enough.
As if most of our protections have not been
removed under this administration.

We fear what will be taken away—
Social Security, Medicare, Medicaid, Disability, Food Stamps,
Affordable Housing, our homes, our freedom.
    Baby boomers often weaken in their fervent
    activism, often wither, often simply tire.

Fear turns outward against immigrants.
ICE builds its detention centers in the middle of
rural communities where most of the workers built
lives in the last twenty years.

ICE rounds up people of color in stores, on city blocks,
hate crimes increase, and the groups behind the crimes
increase in numbers, and use strength, and guns,
    to demolish those they perceive as weaker than they are,
    to use the Second Amendment as their personal protection.

Fear turns inward, and those strong in politics and
    who "resist and persist" though angry,
practice self-care so they can be happy, strong for others, or
escape for a while with podcasts and their own interests.
Since 2016, time is scarce, something happens every day
to intensify fear, to worry about disenfranchised people,
to find the organizations that work the best.

The President, the Congress, the Supreme Court,
now represent the needs of the rich, the desires of the
misogynists and the homophobes. One vote can push back
any progress America has made in attempts for equality,
      for health care for all, for ERA, for all rights.
Change gets pushed back, pushed aside, amidst the myth
that we are the most powerful country.

CATSKILL GREY

It's the kind of weather to avoid,
to live a thousand miles away from
in any direction, but I'm here
for my twenty-fifth high school reunion.
Small pines border
an overcast sky.

A rare truck barrels down
the country road
near my stepdad's trailer,
twenty miles from
where I used to live.

I want to crawl undercover,
under covers,
only come out
when the sun comes out,
only speak when spoken to.

No wonder we rarely went anywhere
as children.
Grey held us in the warmth of home,
making cookies,
playing Scrabble,
listening to the beginning of Motown.

Now I still want
to escape the grey.
I wonder why I'm really here and why,
however strong the wind blows,
the dandelion wisps remain.

Iris Gersh grew up in the Catskills and has lived in Boston where she received a B.A. from Boston University; at the Magic Tortoise 20 miles north of Taos ("in the seventies"); in south Florida; Korinthos, Greece; and since 2005, Albuquerque where she's renewed her love for the high desert. She has an MFA from Florida International University and has taught Sociology, English Composition, and Creative Writing.

While Vice President on the board of the New Mexico State Poetry Society, she organized a poetry mini-workshop as part of New Mexico PBS's screening of Wendell Berry's film, "Kentucky." In 2018, she organized a poetry event at Casa San Ysidro that honored Simon Ortiz where poets shared their own work and poetry of Ortiz. She recently was recognized by the National Federation of State Poetry Societies for her leadership in Youth Poetry Programs.

Her writing has been published in several literary magazines, including the 2017 *Packinghouse Review,* Ekphrastic Issue; the *Alembic*; and *Karamu*. Her story, "Letter to Roland," was chosen for a series of Amazon e-books from Women's Memoir, *Seasons of Our Lives*. Locally, she is published in *Poetry Playhouse Publications; Fixed and Free Anthologies* 2015 and 2018; *Manzano Mountain Review;* and *Best of Dime Stories* online. She is a contributor to *Missing Persons reflections on dementia* from Beatlick Press.

A pre-pandemic highlight was being Feature Poet during Spoken Word at Chatter Sunday's 600th Show in March 2020. She has been involved with readings on Zoom at various venues.

She is an ally for immigration rights groups and social justice causes, and supports protests, resistance, and dissent.

www.ingramcontent.com/pod-product-compliance
Lightning Source LLC
LaVergne TN
LVHW041559070426
835507LV00011B/1188